C0-AJY-230

Moore

WAYNE STATE UNIV.
Bookstores
MONT
0333
$1.80
NOT RETURNABLE
IF LABEL REMOVED

Henry Moore 1955, photograph Roger Wood, London

Universe Sculpture Series

J. P. Hodin

Moore

Universe Books, Inc., New York

The Universe Sculpture Series is edited by Prof. A. M. Hammacher

Library of Congress Catalog Card Number 59-10152
Typography and cover Otto Treumann, GKf, AGI
Printed in the Netherlands by H. Veenman & Zonen N.V., Wageningen

There are no schools in art.
There are only tasks to be mastered.
Edvard Munch

In an age when the conception of man's whole Being, his position in and integration into the Universe, his relationship to powers higher than his own, in short, his inner certainties are shaken; in an age when modern science has deciphered the ambivalent hieroglyphics of man's psyche, when the balance of opposing forces rather than the preoccupation with moral or metaphysical values has become his concern, one must not be astonished to find that the modern artist is not sufficiently attracted either by the realistic portraiture of contemporary man – which indeed could not reveal anything that is not basically queried – or by any imagery which expresses man's relationship to creation and its definition in terms of antiquated notions and beliefs. And both the Christian and the Greek world-view, the idea of the 'new Adam' and that of an idealized humanity expressed in classical canons of beauty, are obsolete today. We need not be distressed about it. It is certain that civilizations are born and die, and it is equally certain that past wisdom is a stage in achieving the wisdom of the future. Everything is in question now, and the reasons for it are obvious. Science is constantly changing not only the state of our consciousness and knowledge, but, above all, and as a direct consequence, life itself around us. This is a slow and painful process. Modern man is striving for a new image of himself and the world, he is in search of his soul. This new image, as we can guess today, will have its roots in the knowledge of the unconscious, it will be defined by the science of phenomena, a global application of it in space and a universal one in time. History and psychology give modern man certainties where mythology gave only symbols and images. On the way towards the new scientific world-view we meet, beside the scientist and the philosopher, the modern artist. It is the modern artist who shapes the images which are significant of this struggle of our consciousness.
Since the Baroque, nothing so decisive has happened in the history of European style as the modern movement. It began with Realism, the return to the natural scene, as opposed to the petrified academic presence of the Christian-Greek-Renaissance conception. Realism already signified modern man's moving towards the roots of Being, and so, where its images are concerned, did Symbolism later, and the return to Primitivity, as well as the suspicion of modern civilization in its materialistic and mechanistic stage. Since then the modern artist has never ceased in his quest to discover new sources of formal inspiration in all the stylistic trends before and beyond the accepted tradition. The really great and new event was Cubism, the complete breach with the traditional way of representation. Cubism is unthinkable without modern science. It is actually its parallel in art. The change of emphasis from physics to biology in science

nowadays corresponds, in art, to the change in emphasis from construction to the principles of organic life, from analytical Cubism to Surrealism, from geometric abstract art to abstract Expressionism.

When Henry Moore emerged with his first mature works – it was about 1923, he was 25 years old – the Cubist spirit which was and still is at the bottom of all courage to radical change and experiment in modern art, had established itself long ago. The Surrealist revolution – with all that this may convey: the a-rational approach to phenomena, the element of surprise, of unexpectedness (objet trouvé), of the primary experience of the subconscious – which had been preparing itself for years, made a new breach into the bastions of obsolete conceptions. In 1925, Breton published his first Manifesto of Surrealism. We shall not find it surprising that his thought, the application to the realm of art of the Freudian findings on the subconscious, meant much to Moore. Although he was never a member of the Surrealist group, he was impelled by its spirit. It was this spirit, too, which released the typically English component of his mind so that his art could develop naturally into that strong manifestation of mastered imagination which after Constable and Turner represents the new contribution England made to modern art. One cannot understand the main obsession of Moore's artistic researches without considering the Englishman's relationship to nature. It was strong enough to influence in outlook a whole age of thought. One only needs to think of the influence of Anthony Ashley Cooper, the first Earl of Shaftesbury's philosophy of nature on Goethe and the German Romantics, or that of the English Garden on the history of European taste, to realize that there was a force which had, in fact, moulded the English mind already in its mythological past. Where Moore stresses the relationships of sculpture and landscape, where he goes so far as to transform the shapes of the human body into characteristics of the landscape itself so that breasts and shoulders and limbs and trunks become mountains and valleys, shores and river-beds and caves, there an old Anglo-Saxon Pantheism breaks through which embraces nature with an elementary need. There also Moore has created his most original works. It is as if a deep stream of inspiration had poured through him, and we suddenly understand what man comes from and where he belongs. Far from attributing to Moore that destructive urge which several authors have recently tried to establish and which, according to them, forces Moore, in following subconscious cruel visions, to dislocate and dismember what is and should remain a whole, we find that his vision in its climax and maturity has revealed to us a greater unity than that represented by purely anthropomorphic imagery.

There is nothing morbid about Moore's phantasy, nothing decadent or purely intellectual. Moore, a son of the working-class – his father was a miner – has a very direct understanding of the work to be done in art. There is no misrepresentation in stating that his is a vision of reality.

For all reality is a convention. It is what we agree to see in it. The problem has two aspects for us: a formal or stylistic one, and one which is concerned primarily with the inner motives of creativeness. The psychologist deals exclusively with the latter aspect, neglecting the other. No psychologist, at least up to now, has been able to give any plausible explanation of Moore's style. In the appreciation of art, we are less concerned with the activity representing the act of creation than with the finished product. The finished product, in art as elsewhere, is governed by formal laws. The modern artist emphasizes that content and form are one. Form has for him its immanent meaning. To read into a work of art psychoanalytical content is as mistaken as to degrade it to the illustration of a literary theme. The art historian who tries to come to grips with the formal problems of modern art, will analyze them from the point of view of stylistic succession and of change. Succession here means: in what way have the new shapes developed out of the old ones, and how does the law of change work according to which art-forms or styles are replaced when the spiritual impetus, which gave birth to them, is exhausted? 'In art there are no schools. There are only tasks to be mastered. Now the turn has come to the *shadows*.' That was Edvard Munch's answer. The *fin de siècle* decadence, the morbidity of Symbolism, the tortured consciousness of the age in which the re-valuation of all values was proclaimed by Nietzsche and the subconscious content of our modern mind started to manifest its restlessness in the works of Goya and Odilon Redon – these were the *shadows* of the underworld in a time which felt that a world of great conceptions was crumbling. In the middle of the twentieth century we feel that a new world is taking shape. Now the turn has come to the inner face of things, to the inner volume, as Moore would say. The outer form in its classic accomplishment cannot be surpassed any more. The artist cannot see any need in trying to continue it. His inner need makes him search for the roots of experience. And he finds inspiration and a similar approach in archaic (Minoan, Cycladic) Greek art; in the Egyptian, the Etruscan or Aztec cultures; in the form-speech of the Primitives; of Negro, Easter Islandic, Sumerian sculptures; of pre-historic works from the dawn of the human mind. The organization of the cell intrigues modern man more than Carlyle's hero worship; the genetic laws, the splitting of the atom, depth psychology more than classic humanism, theological dogma and ethics based on metaphysics. We live in an analytical age, and Moore, as a representative of this age, expresses it in all its aspects. Not Achilles, the Greek ideal, but the Warrior with Shield (ill. no. 28), the body of modern man mutilated by world wars, with a deep gash in his head, battered but proud and not succumbing to dread. The bone structure of living matter (ill. no. 20) rather than the myth of Amor and Psyche, the lower living organisms (ill. no. 17) rather than the Ecce Homo. How nature shapes cavities in cliffs or inside the muscular system in man and animal, how it withers rocks or smoothes pebbles – this is an example and a task for the modern sculptor. For man and rock, the animate and the inanimate, are an expression of the same mysterious force, they are exposed to the onslaught of the same trials. It is not in the idea of harmony as represented in the art of a Phidias or Myron, but in the acceptance of life as a conflict, not in the Romantic idea of nature, but in its real and true face that Moore finds fascination. The hollow form as opposed to the closed form, this is what Moore has explored, together with others. For when the creative freedom of the artist was established by way of the Cubist and Primitivist idea (represented in sculpture by Picasso, Archipenko, Laurens, and, in their early work, also by Lipchitz and Zadkine), the pure constructive form was found (Picasso, Tatlin, Gabo, Pevsner), the imperative demand for the pure organic form stripped of any outdated literary meaning was voiced (Brancusi, Arp), the constructive form was dissolved in its dynamic elements (Boccioni), the negation of volume in sculpture was aimed at (Giacometti). The cavity which hollowed out the form, opened up surprising vistas into surrounding nature, brought the outer space into the inner volume, thus uniting both. This was Henry Moore's special way and achievement. The Greek masters of the Fifth Century B.C. built monuments to the beauty of the human body; Moore builds monuments to the dramatic grandeur of nature. As Picasso made most of his discoveries in a few motifs recurrent in his work – the seated figure and the still-life, around which a few other necessary motifs find their place – so Henry Moore in his vast oeuvre restricted himself basically to two motifs, the Reclining Figure and Mother and Child. To these two motifs correspond two basic stylistic devices: the use of the cavity and the abstracted organic shapes. The principle of concavity was further developed into the interpenetration of outer and inner forms and the creation of a labyrinthic inner space with movements and counter movements. All the other elements of his art find their place in this main scheme.

To be exact, the complete list of Henry Moore's themes would comprise, besides the Mother and Child (Family) motif and the Reclining Figure, Masks, Heads, Heads and Shoulders, Single Figures (standing or seated), Half or Three-Quarter Figures, Compositions (more or less abstract organic carvings and others), Stringed Figures, Two, Three and Four Forms (groups), Two, Three or Four-piece Compositions, Reliefs and Animal Shapes. Of these the Reclining Figures have a small majority over the Single Figures. They are followed by the Mother and Child motif and by the Compositions. The approximate figures are 37 : 36 : 28 : 26. Next, although somewhat remote, come the Two, Three or Four Forms, the Heads, the Stringed Figures, the Half or Three-Quarter Figures, the Two, Three or Four-piece Compositions, the Masks, the Animal Shapes, the Reliefs. Their respective figures are: 17 : 15 : 12 : 12 : 7 : 7 : 5 : 4. Of the main themes, it is that of Mother and Child which preoccupied the artist as early as 1922 and which precedes that of the Reclining Figure. The year 1930 presents the greatest concentration on this motif. The style which it assumes in 1932 has that personal quality which leads directly to the conception of the Madonna and Child in Hornton Stone which Moore produced in 1943–44 as a commission for the Church of St. Matthew in Northampton (ill. no. 9). This was a notable date in the official recognition of modern art for public buildings in England, followed, in 1946, by Graham Sutherland's Crucifixion. Moore himself produced already in 1928 the relief North Wind for the Underground Building at St. James's in London, but this went practically unnoticed. Since 1944 he has received several commissions both in England and abroad, of which the most important are the Memorial Figure for Dartington Hall in South Devon, 1945–46 (ill. no. 10), the Madonna and Child for St. Peter's Church, Claydon, Suffolk, 1943 and 1949, the Family Groups for the Barclay School in Stevenage, Hertfordshire, 1945 and 1949 (ill. no. 13), and for Harlow New Town, Essex, 1944 and 1955. They are followed by the Screen of Four Abstract Figures for the Time/Life Building in London, 1952 (ill. no. 22), and by the Wall Relief in brick, 1954–55 for the Bouwcentrum, Rotterdam (ill. no. 29). Moore is at present working on a monumental composition of three upright forms commissioned for a new building in Milan (ill. no. 30). The Mother and Child theme varies through the years in that it shows the characteristics of Moore's stylistic development until in 1950 it is transmuted into the Rocking Chair motif, giving birth to some remarkable compositions (ill. no. 18), and enlarged into the Family Group motif, 1945–1949. One may assume that we have here to do with a theme which has offered not only compositional points of attraction but one which is connected also with the artist's very personal life. In the case of the Reclining Figure however, we seem to strike a more essential problem, stylistically and psychologically speaking; for here we encounter that stylistic impact which was most decisive on Moore – the Pre-Columbian – and those inner experiences which, according to the writings of different psychologists, seem to be rooted in the deepest layers of his unconscious. Thus, Mr. Frederick S. Wight, from a Freudian viewpoint, speaks of 'the psyche of the child (i.e. the artist's own childhood) wishing and showing the results of the child's activity', in that the chest or breast, the feeding ground of the child, should, from the child's point of view, be eaten away. (The holes.) That is why Moore breaks into the chest cavity, that is why the Reclining Figure of 1945–46 (ill. no. 12) 'reveals a palpable image of some enormous slug (at once foetus, child and lover), burrowing with a teredo-like preoccupation in its inward feeding festival'. The Mother and Child idea and the Reclining Figure are confessed to be one. So much for the Mother implication. The next psychoanalytical symbol evoked – very logically of course – is that of the boneyard. The static quality of Moore's sketches in which the clothes of the figures appear to be cerements, the immovability of his personages, their permanence and eternity, have sepulchral qualities. Does not Moore's working method reflect that of his father – mining – and is not the mine in fact the grave for Moore? The artist is absorbed by the mystery of the living dead because a father image is at work alive underground (see bibl. No. 43).

From a Jungian viewpoint, that is to say in adopting Jungian notions for purposes of interpretation of art without any reference to formal viewpoints and the problem of sequence and change in style and taste, Mr. G. W. Digby tries to explain Henry Moore's peculiar form language (see bibl. No. 27). In essence, the author presupposes the acceptance of the classic Renaissance achievement not only as the starting point of his formal reasoning, but as a generally valid measuring rod, as do those aestheticians for whom, even at the beginning of this century, the classic style was still the only one and the climax of the European development. He can therefore not arrive at any acceptable interpretation of Moore's style. What he does, however, arrive at is what he started with: the appreciation of the Jungian alchemistic-archetypal conception. In terms of cultural-historic and stylistic notions we can come to more tangible results without tearing to pieces what is and must remain a whole, namely the outer happenings and their reflections in man's soul, as well as the formative urge of the artist, an emanation of the living force, and the eternal enigma of life.

It is a mistake to speak of 'psychological factors' instead of the facts of inner experience. Whereas the latter are realized in the work of the artist as a direct result of his living, the former apply only to an intellectual realm, to an academic code of terms. That is also why Mr. Digby's reasoning against Sir Herbert Read and his superimposition of the Jungian notions on formal values, cannot lead to any palpable result. It is highly unsatisfactory to see the individual experience of the artist, both personal and stylistic, pushed into the dark past by an artificial term such as 'the collective unconscious'. There is a hereditary wealth of experience; but there is also what Goethe, as a twenty-year old student, very wisely recognized as contemporaneity. The world for him was 20 years old. The miracle of life is as new a sensation today as it was 3000 years ago. The immense knowledge of history and archeology, of mythology and world-art in our time is certainly no less important than the insistence on introversion. The artist who today looks into a specialist's work on Growth and Form, on Animals Without Backbone, on the Microcosmos of Tissues, can receive as many artistic impulses as any subconscious personal experience can offer. To look for the reasons for destroying the entity of the human body – its 'dismembering' – into psychotic case histories or dream images, is to neglect the present state of world affairs which creates dread and to ignore the problems with which the artist of our time is confronted in accepting science and repudiating traditional formal values which are incapable of expressing the new contents of living. One could go so far as to say that it is an abberation of Jung in his late work and of the Jungians who follow him therein, to emphasize beyond limits the immanent importance of mythology and alchemy for present man and not to consider them in their true relationship to other realms of modern human knowledge.

Although Sir Herbert Read is not altogether free from the same tendency to adapt Jungian

terms to aspects of art, he uses them in a more scholastic manner and never leaves out of sight the formative element, 'the intimate connection between the vitality of art and the deeper significance of form' (see bibl. No. 11).
For us it is deeper, however, not in the sense of Jung but in the sense of the unquenchable thirst for knowledge, the cerebral adventurousness of modern man, his courage, his distrust of all dogma and formula (hence so much in modern art is dead, because it is mere mannerism), his powerful urge to renew himself, his nostalgia to grasp Being (Heidegger), the wholeness of existence (Jaspers), the meaning and spiritual unity of every age and, therefore, also of his own time (Dilthey).
Gestalt psychology again takes another position when analyzing the form speech of Henry Moore (see bibl. No. 44). In its result it comes nearer to that of art criticism than any other psychology. It emphasizes the formal aspect, the shaping, the Gestalt. The reason, according to Mr. Rudolf Arnheim, for the chest to be formed as a large hole, roofed by the shoulders and flanked by the upper arms, must be sought in the modern artist's task not to copy what he sees but to create a whole pattern of unified form. Therefore, he must find a way of imposing unity on so 'heterogeneous' an object as the human body, he must organize the trunk and the limbs in one integrated composition. By transforming the heaviest volume, the trunk, into a configuration of narrower shapes, a common denominator has been found for the whole figure. The beam-like or ribbon-shaped units which represent arms and legs differ little from those which are found in the area of the trunk... etc... Another thought reveals that the holes are not merely dead or empty intervals... equal rights are conceded to hollows and solids. The use of concave forms captures portions of space and makes them a part of the figure. *L'espace limite is replaced by l'espace milieu*, to use a term of Henri Focillon (La Vie des Formes). A more complete survey of spatial relations is thus offered to the spectator. Basing his opinions on the findings of Koffka, amongst others, Mr. Arnheim will comprehend Moore's radical attempt to compose a figure of several entirely separate pieces not as 'dismembering' but as the artistic experiencing of the psychological law that 'perceptual unity does not require physical continuity'.
It is obvious from the contradictory results reached by the different schools of psychology that these interpretations cannot make any claim to being exclusive. What we miss is the totality of a truly human outlook, the knowledge of the balance of powers, inner and outer, conscious and subconscious, of concept and reality.
The Reclining Figure first appeared in Moore's work in 1928. By 1929 it showed the Pre-Columbian impact and developed, by 1930, its first image of identification of human form and landscape. By 1936 the basic conception of 'cavern-making' had matured, leading to that fantastic fiction of 1939 where the landscape aspect is abandoned to cede to the problem of the interpretation of

outer and inner form which we meet in a most convincing way already in the Reclining Figure of 1945-46 and which further leads on the masterpiece of 1953-54 (ill. no. 24), to the Helmet conception for heads (ill. no. 15), and the monumental Internal and External Forms (ill. no. 26). The latter is a masterpiece of composition, filled with vital suggestions. It is subtle as a flower, full as a fruit, mysterious as the life in the womb, as an Egyptian Mummy; a truly poetic rendering of the living powers. This is a work which none but a scientific age could have produced, an age in which the mechanistic and materialistic viewpoint has been defeated and a wider, spiritual one accepted, with a reverence for life and science as its main devotional object.
At the beginning of Moore's career, great importance was given to direct carving. The claims of the material on the formation of the work of art were re-introduced into modern sculpture by Brancusi. Moore, Gaudier-Brzeska, Hepworth, Skeaping, they all adhered to this principle. The succession of stylistic trends confronting our artist in his process of evolution were: the Primitive impact and Animism, the Cubist impact, the Concave-Organic-Abstract impact, the Surrealist impact, and, on and off, Picasso in his chameleon-like metamorphoses. There is also in Moore a genuine understanding of the Mediterranean tradition represented in our time by Marini, Manzu and Greco, and this in turn is closely connected with his traditionally felt approach to sculpture and the calligraphic quality evident throughout his development. His work is neither capricious nor 'shocking' in the sense of the Surrealists but almost always graceful. Unlike Picasso, he retains a Rococo or Botticellian element. In this tendency Moore is supported by an unfailing feeling for proportions. The plastic character is enriched, in his latest phase, by decorative details. (Open-work bronzes, see ill. no. 16.) The great secret of a composition such as King and Queen, 1952–53, which was acquired by the Middleheim Park Collection in Antwerp, lies precisely in the combination of both the archaic and the vital, i.e. the primary on the one hand and the pleasing, the decorative, even narrative element on the other. Without intention, a work of symbolic essence was here created: the absolute and abstract quality of 'kingdom'. The age-old institution of kingship is expressed in bone-like heads placed on elongated archaic trunks with crowns growing as organically as the inner structure of bodies. This combination of different qualities mastered by a supreme taste is also the reason for Moore's popularity. A manifold unity is here achieved which might be compared to that of Shakespeare's plays where the tragic is balanced by the comic, the significant by eloquence. The 'serial' production of some of Moore's later works again has its reason in this popularity.
Moore's sculptural vision is a formal not a symbolic one. Whenever he deviates, and this happens very rarely, into a 'sadistic' extreme, he does so more for reasons of modern formal orthodoxy than of subconscious Expressionism. In the final adjustment of bold experimental ideas to those of a more tradition-bound quality (the Family Group, King and Queen, Warrior with Shield) a

great achievement is visible. For today it is not difficult to 'run wild' in art; today it is more difficult not to do so.
At the base of Moore's art lies a deeply founded artistic and human curiosity. That is why, satiated with the formalistic approach, he tries out in his recent phase, both the amorphous. the Mediaeval and the direct incorporation of natural objects into his sculpture (ill. no. 29). That is also why he challenges classic Greek art in its masterly use of drapery (ill. no. 23), But what a difference in result! It is the difference between idealism and beauty, and the Darwinian concept of life. The insistence on the disturbing element in life, on struggle, stands in absolute opposition to the Classic view. For this reason, Moore's style cannot be 'perfectionist' in the sense of Greek or Chinese Classicism – it is consciously anti-perfectionist.

Notes of the artist

Primitive art

'The most striking quality common to all primitive art is its intense vitality. It is something made by people with a direct and immediate response to life. Sculpture and painting for them was not an activity of calculation or academism, but a channel for expressing powerful beliefs, hopes and fears. It is art before it got smothered in trimmings and surface decorations, before inspiration had flagged into technical tricks and intellectual conceits. But apart from its own enduring value, a knowledge of it conditions a fuller and truer appreciation of the later developments of the so-called great periods, and shows art to be a universal continuous activity with no separation between past and present.
All art has its roots in the 'primitive', or else it becomes decadent, which explains why the 'great' periods, Pericles' Greece and the Renaissance for example, flower and follow quickly on primitive periods, and then slowly fade out'. Underlying the individual characteristics and featural peculiarities of the different primitive schools, 'a common world language of form is apparent...; through the working of instinctive sculptural sensibility, the same shapes and form relationships are used to express similar ideas at widely different places and periods in history, so that the same form-vision may be seen in a Negro and a Viking carving, a Cycladic stone figure and a Nukuoro wooden statuette... It eventually became clear to me that the realistic ideal of physical beauty in art which sprang from fifth-century Greece was only a digression from the main world tradition of sculpture, whilst, for instance, our own equally European Romanesque and Early Gothic are in the main line.'

The Listener, London, Vol. XXV, No. 641, pp. 598–599. April 24th, 1941

The sculptor's aims

Truth to material. *'Every material has its own individual qualities. It is only when the sculptor works direct, when there is an active relationship with his material, that the material can take its part in the shaping of an idea.'*

Full three-dimensional realization. *'Complete sculptural expression is form in its full spatial reality.*
Only to make relief shapes on the surface of the block is to forgo the full power of expression of sculpture.'
'Sculpture fully in the round has no two points of view alike. The desire for form completely realized is connected with asymmetry. For a symmetrical mass being the same from both sides cannot have more than half the number of different points of view possessed by a non-symmetrical mass.
'Asymmetry is connected also with the desire for the organic (which I have) rather than the geometric.'

Observation of natural objects. *'The observation of nature is part of an artist's life, it enlarges his form-knowledge, keeps him fresh and from working only by formula, and feeds inspiration.*
The human figure is what interests me most deeply, but I have found principles of form and rhythm from the study of natural objects such as pebbles, rocks, bones, trees, shells, etc.'
'Pebbles and rocks show nature's way of working stone. Smooth, sea-worm pebbles show the wearing away, rubbed treatment of stone and principles of asymmetry.
Rocks show the hacked, hewn treatment of stone, and have a jagged nervous block rhythm.
Bones have marvellous structural strength and hard tenseness of form, subtle transition of one shape into the next and great variety in section.
Trees (tree trunks) show principles of growth and strength of joints, with easy passing of one section into the next. They give the ideal for wood sculpture, upward twisting movement.
Shells show nature's hard but hollow form (metal sculpture) and have a wonderful completeness of single shape.'

Vision and expression. *'My aim in work is to combine, as intensely as possible, the abstract principles of sculpture along with the realization of my idea...*
Abstract qualities of design are essential to the value of a work, but to me of equal importance is the psychological, human element. If both abstract and human elements are welded together in a work, it must have a fuller, deeper meaning.'

Vitality and power of expression. *'For me a work must first have a vitality of its own. I do not mean a reflection of the vitality of life, of movement, physical action, frisking, dancing figures and so on, but that a work can have in it a pent-up energy, an intense life of its own, independent of the object it may represent...*
Beauty, in the later Greek or Renaissance sense, is not the aim of my sculpture.
Between beauty of expression and power of expression there is a difference of function. The first aims at pleasing the senses, the second has a spiritual vitality which for me is more moving and goes deeper than the senses.'

Unit One, p. 128; Edit. by Herbert Read, London, 1934

Brancusi

'Since the Gothic, European sculpture had become over-grown with moss, weeds – all sorts of surface excrescences which completely concealed shape. It has been Brancusi's special mission to get rid of this overgrowth, and to make us once more shape-conscious. To do this he has had to concentrate on very simple direct shapes, to keep his sculpture, as it were, one-cylindred, to refine and polish a single shape to a degree almost too precious. Brancusi's work, apart from its individual value, has been of historical importance in the development of contemporary sculpture. But it may now be no longer necessary to close down and restrict sculpture to the single (static) form unit. We can now begin to open out. To relate and combine together several forms of varied sizes, sections and directions into one organic whole...'

Holes

'A piece of stone can have a hole through it and not be weakened – if the hole is of a studied size, shape and direction. On the principle of the arch, it can remain just as strong.
The first hole made through a piece of stone is a revelation.
The hole connects one side to the other, making it immediately more three-dimensional.
A hole can itself have as much shape-meaning as a solid mass...
The mystery of the hole – the mysterious fascination of caves in hillsides and cliffs.'

Drawings

'My drawings are done mainly as a help towards making sculpture – as a means of generating ideas for sculpture, tapping oneself for the initial idea; and as a way of sorting out ideas and developing them. Also, sculpture compared with drawing is a slow means of expression, and I find drawing a useful outlet

for ideas which there is not time enough to realize as sculpture. And I use drawing as a method of study and observation of natural forms (drawings from life, drawings of bones, shells, etc.). And I sometimes draw just for its own enjoyment.
Experience though has taught me that the difference there is between drawing and sculpture should not be forgotten. A sculptural idea which may be satisfactory as a drawing always needs some alteration when translated into sculpture.'

Abstractionists and surrealists

'The violent quarrel between the abstractionists and the surrealists seems to me quite unnecessary. All good art has contained both abstract and surrealist elements, just as it has contained both classical and romantic elements – order and surprise, intellect and imagination, conscious and unconscious. Both sides of the artist's personality must play their part.'

All quoted from The Painter's Object,
pp. 21–29; Edit. by Myfanwy Evans, London, 1937

Sculpture and architecture

'Purely abstract thinking is a matter of taste and design, it is not sculpture. Did it strike you how lifeless such a sculpture seems in front of architecture? Instead of stressing the contrast, organic forms – architectural forms, these two architectural conceptions kill each other. I dropped all this very quickly.'

Quoted from J. P. Hodin: Henry Moore,
World Review, London, August, 1949, p. 153

The artist and modern society

'There have been periods – periods which we would like to regard as ideal prototypes of society – in which that relationship was simple. Society had a unified structure, whether communal or hierarchic, and the artist was a member of that society with a definite place and a definite function. There was a universal faith, and an accepted interplay of authority and function which left the artist with a defined task, and a secure position. Unfortunately our problems are not simplified in that way. We have a society which is fragmented, authority which resides in no certain place, and our function as artists is what we make it by our individual efforts. We live in a transitional age, between one economic structure of society which is in dissolution and another economic order of society which has not yet taken definite shape. As artists we do not know who is our master; we are individuals seeking patronage,

sometimes from another individual, sometimes from an organization of individuals – a public corporation, a museum, an educational authority – sometimes from the State itself. This very diversity of patronage requires, on the part of the modern artist, an adaptability or agility that was not required of the artist in a unified society.'

'It is the fundamental truth to which we must always return – that culture (as the word implies) is an organic process. There is no such thing as synthetic culture, or if there is, it is a false and impermanent culture. Nevertheless, on the basis of our knowledge of the history of art, on the basis of our understanding of the psychology of the artist, we know that there are certain social conditions that favour the growth and flourishing of art, others that destroy or inhibit that growth.'

Quoted from The Artist in Modern Society,
International Conference of Artists,
Venice, 22–28 September, 1952, pp. 97–102, Unesco, Paris, 1954

Chronology

Life Data

1898 July 30. Born at Castleford, Yorkshire, a mining town near Leeds.

1910 Won a scholarship from his elementary school to Castleford Grammar School.

1915 Became a student-teacher –despite his ambition to be a sculptor.

1917 Joined up in February as a private in the 15th London Regiment (Civil Service Rifles). Went to France in the early summer. Gassed in the Battle of Cambrai.

1919 Was demobilized in February and entered the Leeds School of Art.

1921 Won a Royal Exhibition Scholarship in Sculpture, and in September entered the Roya College of Art.

1925 Awarded Royal College of Art Travelling Scholarship; was appointed instructor in the Sculpture School for a term of seven years.

1926 Spent six months abroad visiting Paris, Rome, Florence, Padua, Ravenna, and Venice.

1928 Received first public commission.

1932 Exhibited at the Chelsea School of Art.

1933 Becomes Member of 'Unit One'.

1936 Participated in the International Surrealist Exhibition in London. Saw cave-paintings in the Pyrenees and at Altamira, and visited Madrid, Toledo, and Barcelona.

1939 Gave up art teaching.

1940 Began making shelter drawings and was appointed official war artist.

1941 Appointed a Trustee of the Tate Gallery.

1945 Appointed a member of the Art Panel of the Arts Council. Created Honorary Doctor of Literature at the University of Leeds. First post-war visit to Paris in November.

1946 Visited New York on the occasion of his exhibition at the Museum of Modern Art, his first retrospective exhibition.

1948 Appointed a member of the Royal Fine Arts Commission. Elected Honorary Associate of the Royal Institute of British Architects. Elected Foreign Corresponding Member of the Academie Royale Flammande des Sciences, Lettres et Beaux-Arts de Belgique. Awarded the International Sculpture Prize at the 24th Venice Biennale. Visited Florence, Pisa and Venice.

1949 Visited Brussels, Amsterdam, and Berne.

1951 Elected a foreign member of the Swedish Royal Academy of Fine Arts.

1952 Visited Florence and Rome.

1953 Created Honorary Doctor of Literature at the University of London. Awarded the International Prize for Sculpture at the 2nd São-Paulo Biennal. Visited Brazil and Mexico.

1954 Visited Milan, Venice, Rome, Rotterdam, and Hanover.

1955 Elected Foreign Honorary Member of the American Academy of Arts and Sciences. Appointed a Trustee of the National Gallery. Appointed member of the Order of the Companions of Honour. Visited Yugoslavia and the Ruhr.

Exhibitions

1927 Exhibited for the first time in a mixed show in London

1928 London.

1931 London.

1933 London.

1935 London.

1936 London.

1939 London.

1940 London.

1941 Leeds.

1943 New York.

1945 London.

1946 London. Washington, Philips Memorial Gallery. New York, Museum of Modern Art.

Chicago, Art Institute of Chicago. San Francisco, Museum of Modern Art. Sydney, National Gallery of New South Wales. Hobart, Tasmanian Museum and Art Gallery. Melbourne, National Gallery of Victoria. Adelaide, National Gallery of South Australia, Perth, National Gallery of Western Australia.

1948 Cambridge. Venice. Milan, Galleria d'Arte Moderna. London.

1949 Wakefield. Manchester. Brussels, Palais des Beaux Arts. Paris, Musée Nationale d'Art Moderne.

1950 Amsterdam, Stedelijk Museum. Hamburg, Kunsthalle. Dusseldorf, Städtische Kunstsammlungen. Berne, Kunsthalle. Mexico City, Galeria de Arte Mexicano. Guadalajara.

1951 Athens. London, Tate Gallery. London. Berlin. New York. Vienna, Albertina.

1952 Cape Town, National Gallery of South Africa. Stockholm. Norrköping. Örebro. Göteborg. Linz. Stockholm.

1953 Copenhagen. Oslo. Trondheim. Bergen. Rotterdam. London, Institute of Contemporary Arts. Antwerp. Hanover. Munich. Frankfurt. Stuttgart. São Paulo.

1954 London. Mannheim, Künsthalle. Bremen, Künsthalle. Berlin. Göttingen. New York.

1955 Basle, Kunsthalle. Colorado, Colorado Springs Fine Art Center. Denver, Denver Art Museum. Wyoming. Zagreb. Belgrade. Llubljana.

Selected Bibliography

The complete bibliography of books, articles and catalogues in practically all major languages- comprised more than 310 items by the end of 1955.

Books

1 Henry Moore — *Sculpture and Drawings*. With an Introduction by Herbert Read. Essays by the artist, and Bibliography. 55 pp. text and 25 illustrations. 260 plates of which one coloured. Lund Humphries & Co, Ltd., A. Zwemmer, London, 3rd revised and enlarged edition 1949.

2 Henry Moore — Volume 2. *Sculpture and Drawings since 1948*. With an Introduction by Herbert Read, Observations by the artist, and Bibliography- 24 pp. text and 7 illustrations. 117 plates in black and white. Lund Humphries & Co. Ltd., A. Zwemmer, London, 1955.

Some Statements by Moore in:

3 *Unit One* — *The Modern Movement in English Architecture, Painting and Sculpture*, (edited by Herbert Read), London, 1934.

4 *Circle* — *International Survey of Constructive Art*, London, 1937.

5 *The Listener* — London, Vol. 18, No. 449, 1937; Vol. 25, No. 641, 1941; Vol. 26, No. 670, 1941.

6 *Art News* — *The Sculptor in Modern Society*, New York, Vol. 5, No. 6, 1952.

7 *Sculpture in the Open Air* — a Talk by Henry Moore on his Sculpture and its placing in open-air sites. Edited by Robert Melville and specially recorded, with accompanying illustrations, by the British Council, London, 1955.

8 Herbert Read — *The Meaning of Art*, London, 1931, pp. 148–153.

9 — *Henry Moore, Sculptor*, A. Zwemmer, London, 1934.

10 — *The Philosophy of Modern Art*, London, 1952, pp. 195–215.

11 — *The Dynamics of Art*, in: Eranos Jahrbuch, XXI, Zürich, 1953 pp. 225–284.

12 Paul Fierens — *Sculpture d'Aujourdhui*, Paris-London, 1953, p. 19.

13 C. Giedion-Welcher, — *Modern Plastic Art*, Zürich, 1937, pp. 12, 110–111, 157.

14 — *Contemporary Sculpture*, revised edition, New York, 1953.

15 Christopher Blake — *Modern English Art*, London, 1937, pp. 76–77.

16 R. Ironside — *Painting Since 1939*, London-New York, 1939.

17 Geoffrey Grigson — *Henry Moore*, Penguin Books, 1943, Harmondsworth, Middlesex

18 J. H. Sweeney, — *Henry Moore*, New York, 1946.

19 W. R. Valentiner — *Origins of Modern Sculpture*, New York, 1946.

20 G. C. Argan — *Henry Moore*, Torino, 1948.

21 A. C. Ritchie — *Sculpture of the Twentieth Century*, New York, 1952, pp. 41, 124–129, 192–195.

22 E. H. Ramsden — Sculpture: *Theme and Variations*, London, 1953, p. 41 seq.

23 N. Gertz — *Plastik der Gegenwart*, Berlin, 1953, pp. 20–22, 196–203, 218, 222–223.

24 H. Felix Man — *Eight European Artists*, London, 1954, section 6.

25 Alfred H. Barr, Jr. — *Masters of Modern Art*, New York, 1954, pp. 45, 105, 148, 149.

26 Eric Newton — *In my View*, London-New York-Toronto, 1954, pp. 41–44.

27 G. W. Digby — *Meaning and Symbol in Three Modern Artists*, London, 1955, pp. 61–105.

28 Patrick Heron — *The Changing Forms of Art*, London, 1955, pp. 208–215.

29 J. P. Hodin — *The Dilemma of Being Modern*, London, 1956, pp. 99–105, first published in World Review, London, August, 1949.

Articles

30 Reginald Howard Wilenski — 'Ruminations on Sculpture and the Work of Henry Moore' *Apollo*, London, December 1930.

31 Denys Sutton — 'Henry Moore and the English Tradition', *Kingdom Come*, Oxford, Winter 1941–41.

32 Peggy Guggenheim — 'Art of This Century', New York, *Art of This Century*, 1942.

33 Philip Hendy — 'Henry Moore', *Britain To-Day*, London, February 1945.

34 Nikolaus Pevsner — 'Thoughts on Henry Moore', *Burlington Magazine*, London, February, 1945.

35 James Thrall Soby — 'Art in England Today', *Saturday Review of Literature*, New York, December 17, 1946.

36 J. P. Hodin — 'Henry Moore', *Paletten*, Gothenburg, No. 3, 1947.

37 — 'Henry Moore', *Kronick van Kunst en Kultur*, Amsterdam, Vol. 11, No. 1, 1950, pp. 1–5.

38 — 'Recent Trends in Contemporary English Sculpture and Their Origins', *Aesthetics*, International Art Numbert, Bombay, no date. Reprinted in *Sele Arte*, Florence, No. 9, 1953, pp. 57–66, with an art historic comment by Prof. Carlo L. Ragghianti.

39 — 'Conversations with Henry Moore', *Quadrum*, No. 1, Brussels, April, 1956.

40 Ralph M. Pearson — 'Moore, Positive and Negative', *Art Digest*, New York, March 15, 1947.

41 Gigi Richter — 'Introduction to Henry Moore', *Art in America*, Springfield, Mass., January 1947.

42 James Johnson Sweeney — 'Interview with Henry Moore', *Partisan Review*, New York, March-April, 1947.

43 Frederich S. Wight — 'Henry Moore: The Reclining Figure', *Journal of Aesthetics and Art Criticism*, Baltimore, December, 1947.

44 Rudolf Arnheim — 'The Holes of Henry Moore', *Journal of Aesthetics and Art Criticism*, Baltimore, September, 1948.

45 Robert Melville — 'Contemporary Sculpture in the Open Air', *The Listener*, London, June 10, 1948.

46 A. D. B. Sylvester, — 'Evolution of Henry Moore's Sculpture', *Burlington Magazine*, London, June-July, 1948.

47 — 'Henry Moore's Sculpture', *Britain Today*, March, 1954.

48 Leon Degand — 'Henry Moore', *Art d'Aujourdhui*, Paris, November, 1949.

49 Robert Vrinat — 'L'Evolution de la Figure couchée dans l'Oeuvre de Henry Moore' *L'Age Nouveau*, Paris, November, 1949.

50 Margaret Underwood — 'Vernieuwer der Beeldhouwkunst', *Kronick van Kunst en Kultuur*, Amsterdam, January, 1950.

51 Kenneth Clark — 'Henry Moore's Metal Sculpture', *Magazine of Art*, New York, May, 1951.

52 Ferdinand Finne — 'Henry Moore', *Kunsten Idag*, Oslo, Vol. 18, No. 2–3, 1951.

53 Waldemar George — 'Les Silences d'Henry Moore', *Art et Industrie*, Paris, January, 1952.

54 Michael Middleton — 'Henry Moore', *L'Oeil*, Paris, March 15, 1955.

55 Mario Negri, — 'Henry Moore', *Domus*, Milan, September, 1955.

Catalogues

British Council, London, *Exhibition of Sculpture and Drawings by Henry Moore to be shown at the State Galleries of Sydney, Hobart, Melbourne, Adelaide, Perth*, Melbourne, 1947
Sculptures and Drawings by Henry Moore, Venice, Biennale, 1948

British Institute of Adult Education, London, *3 British Artists: Henry Moore, John Piper, Graham Sutherland: Exhibition Catalogue*, London, 1947

Buchholz Gallery, Curt Valentin, New York, *Henry Moore, 40 Watercolors and Drawings*, New York, 1943
The Drawings of Henry Moore, New York, 1946

Hamburg, Kunsthalle, and Düsseldorf, Städtische Kunstsammlungen: *Henry Moore: Ausstellung von Skulpturen und Zeichnungen*, 1950
Introduction by Herbert Read, Statement by Moore

Paris, Musée National d'Art Moderne, *Henry Moore*, Paris, 1949
Introduction by Herbert Read

Rotterdam Boymans Museum, *Henry Moore*, Rotterdam, 1953
With a Statement by Moore and Introduction by Philip Hendy

São Paulo Museu de Arte Moderna, *Gra-Bretanha: Esposicao de Obras de Moore, Richards, Evans, Scott, Gear, Heron*, São Paulo, 1953

Illustrations

1	**Masque**	béton	57cm	1928	collection privée
	Mask	concrete	18½ ins.		private collection
	Maske	Beton			Privatbesitz
	Masker	beton			particuliere verzameling

2 **Figure**	béton	40½ cm	1929	coll. British Council & Sir Phillip Hendy
Figure	concrete	16 ins.		
Figur	Beton			
Figuur	beton			
Figura	cemento			

3 **Figure appuyée**	albâtre	46 cm	1929	coll. Mrs. Wertheim
Reclining figure	alabaster	18 ins.		
Liegende Figur	Alabaster			
Achterover leunende figuur	albast			
Figura reclinada	alabastro			

4	**Mère et enfant** **Mother and child** **Mutter und Kind** **Moeder en Kind** **Madre e hijo**	verde di prato	2,44 m 8 ft.	1930	coll. Sir Eric Maclagan

5	**Deux formes**	bois africain	56 cm	1934	Museum of Modern Art, New York
	Two forms	african wood	22 ins.		
	Zwei Formen	Afrikanisches Holz			
	Twee vormen	Afrikaans hout			
	Dos formas	madera africana			

6	**Composition en quatre pièces**	figure allongée	Cumberland	albâtre	50.8 cm	1934
	Four-piece composition	reclining figure	Cumberland	alabaster	20 ins.	
	Vierteilige Komposition	liegende Figur	Cumberland	Alabaster		
	Compositie in vier stukken	liggende figuur	Cumberland	albast		
		coll. Miss Lois Orswell, Narragausett, Rhode Island				
	Composición en cuatro partes	figura reclinada	alabastro Cumberland			

7 **Figure**	marbre	48 cm	1937	coll. A. Lancaster Lloyd
Figure	Birds eye marble	19 ins.		
Figur	Marmor			
Figuur	marmer			
Figura	mármol			

8	**Figure**	plomb et fil de fer	28 cm	1939	coll. Mrs. H. Lampard
	Figure	lead and wire	11 ins.		
	Figur	Blei und Draht			
	Figuur	lood en staaldraad			
	Figura	plomo y alambre			

9	**Madone et enfant**	bronze	1.50 m	1943–44	coll. Church of St. Mathew
	Madonna and child	bronze	4 ft. 11 ins.		Northhampton
	Madonna mit Kind	Bronze			
	Madonna met kind	brons			
	La Virgen y el Niño	bronce			

10	**Figure d'un mémorial**		1.42 m	1945–46	Dartington Hall,
	Memorial figure	horton stone	56 ins.		Devon, England
	Denkmalsfigur				
	Figuur van Herdenkingsmonument				
	Figura recordatoria				

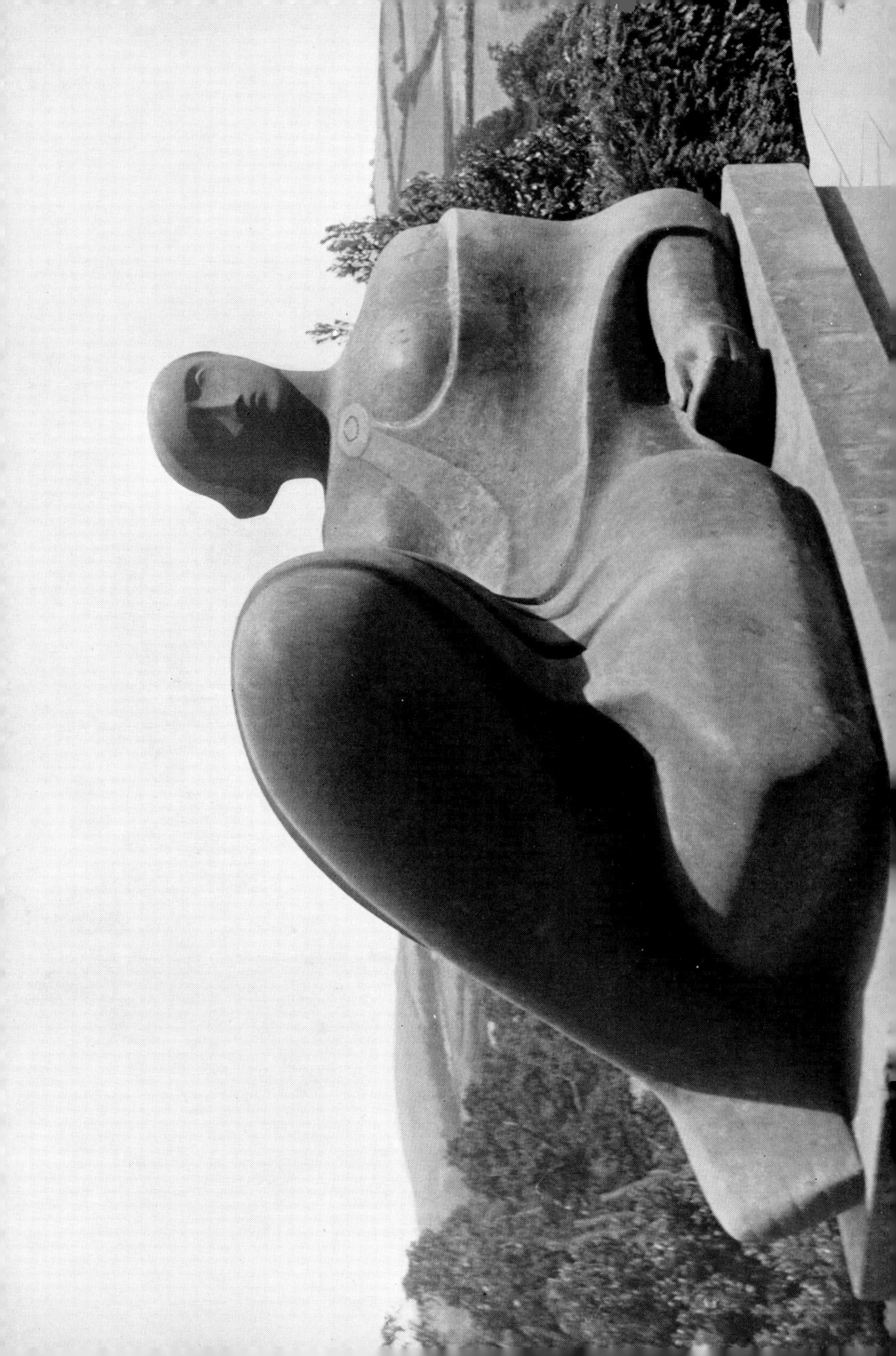

11	**Figure appuyée no. 1**	1945	bronze, version polie	40.5 cm	collection privée
	Reclining figure no. 1		bronze, polished version	16 ins.	private collection
	Liegende Figur Nr. 1		Bronze, polierte Version		Privatbesitz
	Achterover leunende figuur nr. 1		brons, gepolijste versie		particuliere verzameling
	Figura reclinada No. 1		bronce, versión pulida		colección privada

12 **Figure appuyée**	bois d'orme	1,90 m	1945–46	coll. Cranbrook Academy of Art,
Reclining figure	elm	75 ins.		Bloomfield Hills. Mich. U.S.A.
Liegende Figur	Ulme			
Achterover leunende figuur	iepenhout			
Figura reclinada	madera de olmo			

13	**Groupe de famille**	bronze	1.52 m	1945–49	Barclay school, Stevenage, England
	Family group	bronze	60 ins.		
	Familiengruppe	Bronze			
	Familiegroep	brons			
	Grupo familiar	bronce			

14	**Trois figures debout**		2.13 m	1947–48	Battersea Park, London
	Three standing figures	Darley Dak stone	84 ins.		
	Drei stehende Figuren				
	Drie staande figuren				
	Tres figuras de pie				

15	**Tête avec casque no. 2**	bronze	35,5 cm	1950	collection privée
	Helmet head no. 2	bronze	14 ins.		private collection
	Kopf mit Helm Nr. 2	Bronze			Privatbesitz
	Gehelmde kop nr. 2	brons			particuliere verzameling
	Cabeza con casco No. 2	bronce			colección privada

16	**Tête**	maquette	bronze	14 cm	1950	coll. Arthur Jeffries
	Head	model	bronze	$5\frac{1}{4}$ ins.		
	Kopf	Entwurf	Bronze			
	Kop	ontwerp	brons			
	Cabeza	maqueta	bronce			

17	**Tête animale**	bronze	hauteur	21.5 cm	1951	collection privée
	Animal head	bronze		$8\frac{1}{2}$ ins. high		private collection
	Tierkopf	Bronze				Privatbesitz
	Dierekop	brons				particuliere verzameling
	Cabeza de animal	bronce				colección privada

18	**Fauteuil à bascule**	no. 3	bronze	32 cm	1950	collection privée
	Rocking chair		bronze	12½ ins.		private collection
	Schaukelstuhl		Bronze			Privatbesitz
	Schommelstoel		brons			particuliere verzameling
	La mecedora		bronce			colección privada

19	**Figure appuyée**	bronze	2.28 cm	1951	Arts Council
	Reclining figure	bronze	7 ft. 6 ins.		
	Liegende Figur	Bronze			
	Achterover leunende figuur	brons			
	Figura reclinada	bronce			

20	**Figure debout**	bronze	2.21 cm	1950	coll. W. J. Keswick, Dumfries, Scotland
	Standing figure	bronze	7 ft. 3 ins.		
	Stehende Figur	Bronze			
	Staande figuur	brons			
	Figura de pie	bronce			

21	**Roi et reine**	bronze	1.64 m	1952–53	coll. W. J. Keswick,
	King and queen	bronze	5 ft. 4½ ins.		Dumfries, Scotland
	König und Königin	Bronze			
	Koning en koningin	brons			
	Rey y reina	bronce			

22	**Cloison**		8.08 × 3.04 m	1952–53	Time/Life Building,
	Screen	Portland Stone	26 ft. 6 ins. × 10 ft.		Bond Street, London
	Zaun				
	Hekwerk				
	Pantalla para chimenea				

23	**Figure drapée, appuyée**	detail	bronze	1.57 cm	1952–53	Time/Life Building,
	Draped reclining figure	detail	bronze	5 ft. 2 ins.		Bond Street, London
	Bekleidete liegende Figur	Detail	Bronze			
	Beklede achterover leunende figuur	detail	brons			
	Figura reclinada con manto	detalle	bronce			

24	**Figure appuyée**	forme extérieure	bronze	2.13 m	1953–54	collection privée
	Reclining figure	external form	bronze	7 ft.		private collection
	Liegende Figur	äussere Form	Bronze			Privatbesitz
	Achterover leunende figuur	uitwendige vorm	brons			particuliere verzameling
	Figura reclinada	forma exterior	bronce			colección privada

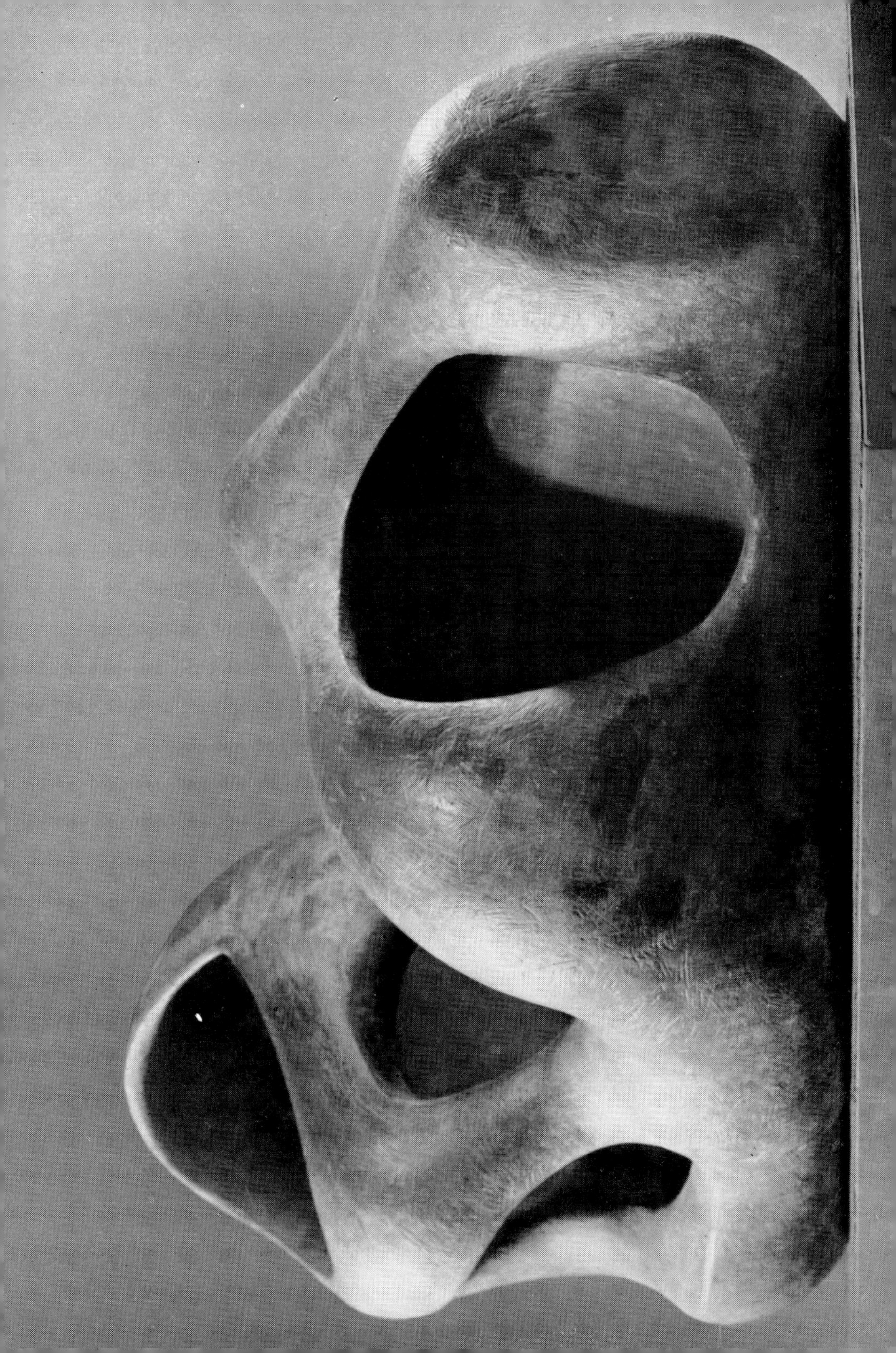

25	**Figure appuyée**	forme extérieure, detail	bronze	1953–54	2.13 m
	Reclining figure	external form, detail	bronze		7 ft
	Liegende Figur	äussere Form, Detail	Bronze		
	Achterover liggende figuur	detail van de buitenkant	brons		
	Figura reclinada	forma exterior, detalle	bronce		

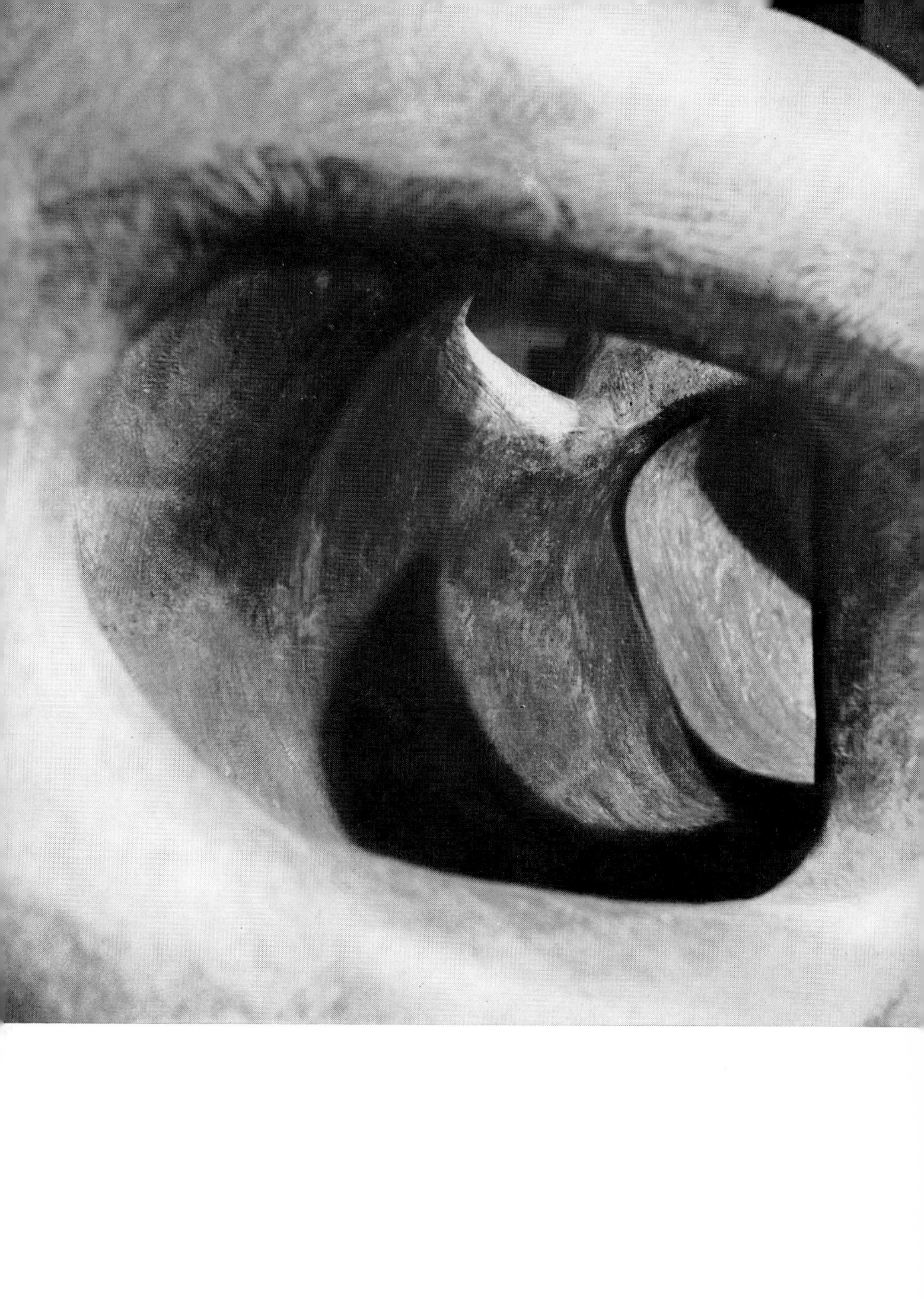

26	**Formes intérieures et extérieures**	bois d'orme	2.63 m	1953–54	Albright Art Gallery,
	Internal and external forms	elm wood	8 ft. $7\frac{1}{4}$ ins.		Buffalo, U.S.A.
	Innere und äussere Formen	Ulme			
	Inwendige en uitwendige vormen	iepenhout			
	Formas interiores y exteriores	madera de olmo			

27	**Formes intérieures et extérieures**	detail	bois d'orme	2.63 m	1953–54	Albright Art
	Internal and external forms	detail	elm wood	8 ft./¼ ins. high		Gallery, Buffalo,
	Innere und äussere Formen	Detail	Ulme			U.S.A.
	Inwendige en uitwendige vormen	detail	iepenhout			
	Formas interiores y exteriores	detalle	madera de olmo			

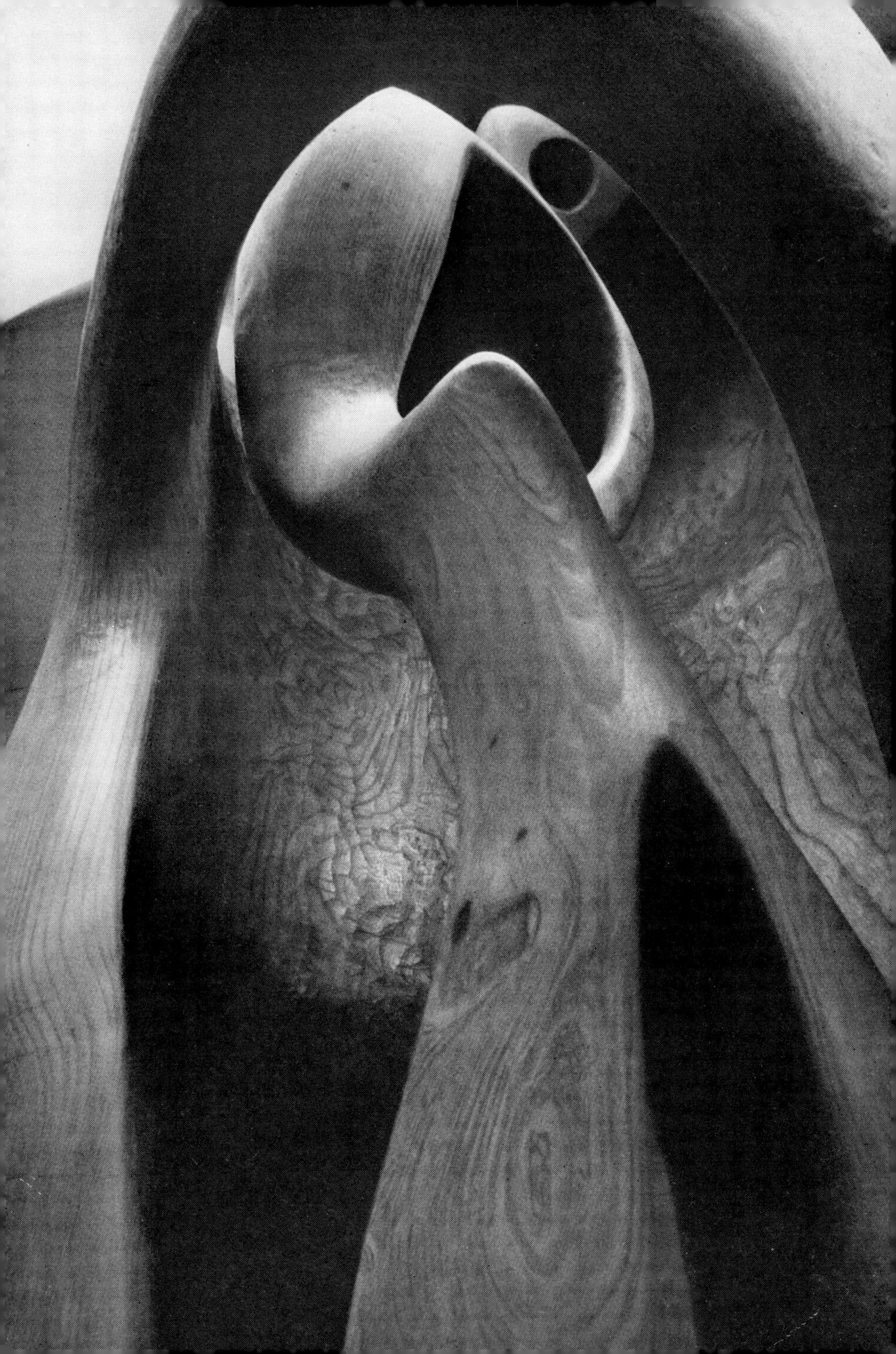

28	**Guerrier avec bouclier**	bronze	1,52 m	Art Gallery, Toronto, Canada
	Warrior with shield	bronze	5 ft	
	Krieger mit Schild	Bronze		
	Krijger met schild	brons		
	Guerrero con escudo	bronce		

29a + b **Maquette en plâtre et réalisation en brique d'un mur-reliëf** 1955 Bouwcentrum, Rotterdam
Model in plaster and its for a realization in brick wall-relief
Entwurf in Gips für ein Wandrelief und seine Ausführung aus Ziegelstein
Ontwerp in gips voor een muurreliëf en de uitvoering in baksteen
Maqueta en yeso y su ejecución en ladrillo de un relieve mural

30 **Maquettes en plâtre pour une composition de trois formes debout pour Milan** 1955–56
Models in plaster for monumental composition of three upright forms for Milan
Entwürfe in Gips für eine Komposition von drei aufrechten Formen für Mailand
Ontwerpen in gips voor een compositie van drie rechtopstaande vormen voor Milaan
Maquetas en yeso para una composición de tres formas de pie para Milán

31	**Abri antiaérien**	plume et aquarelle	1941	42.5 × 38 cm	Tate Gallery, London
	Tilbury shelter	pen and watercolour		$16\frac{3}{4}$ × 15 ins.	
	Luftschutzraum	Federzeichnung und Aquarell			
	Schuilkelder	pentekening en aquarel			
	Refugio antiaéreo	pluma y acuarela			

32	**Groupes de famille**	crayon, plume et aquarelle	48 × 35.5 cm	1944	coll. Gill Graigie
	Family groups	chalk, pen and watercolours	19 × 14 ins.		
	Familiengruppen	Kreide, Feder und Aquarell			
	Familie-groepen	krijt, pen en aquarel			
	Grupo familiar	pluma y acuarela			

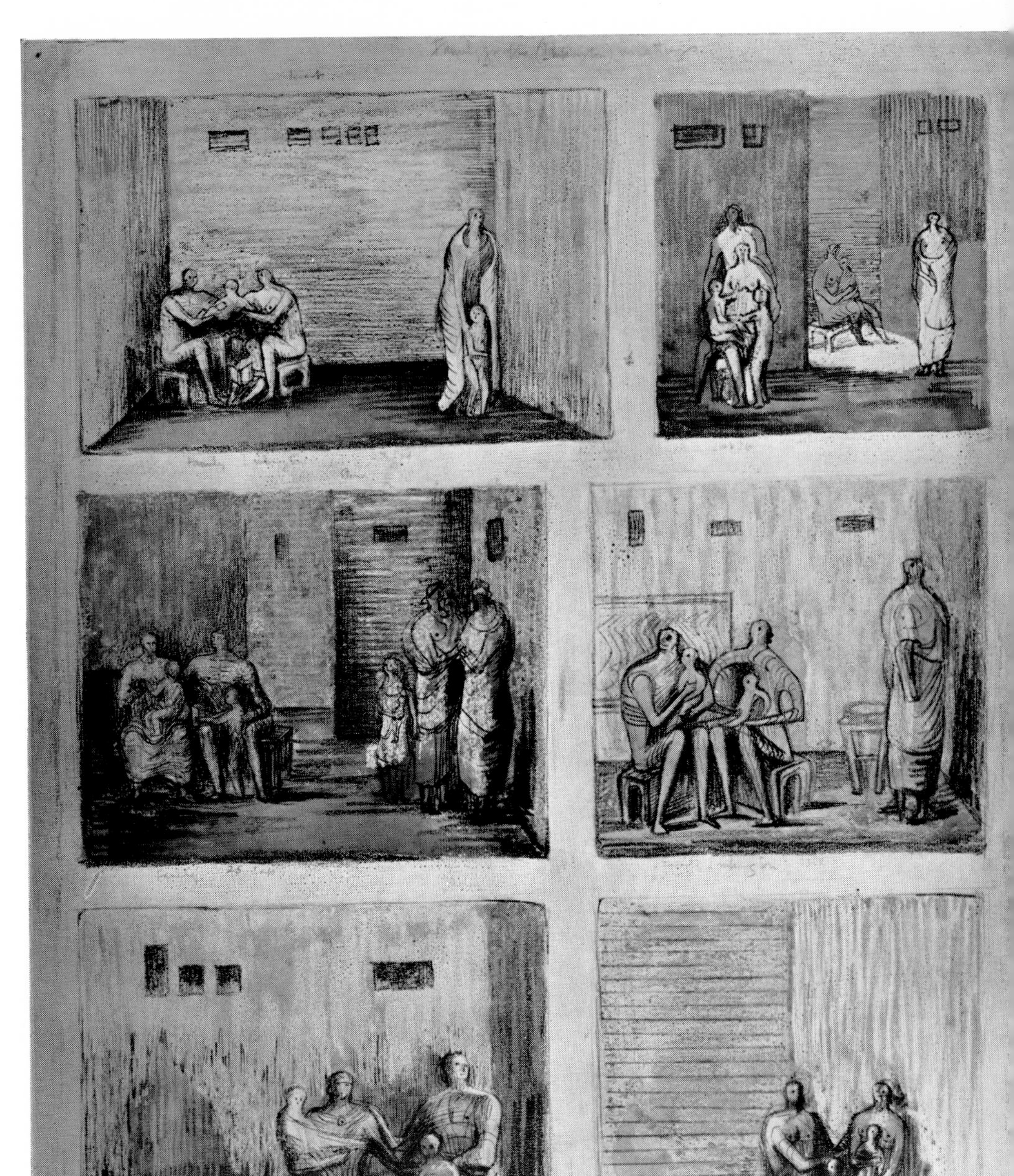
Moore
44